A Sort of Adam Infant Dropped:

True Myths

R. Scott Yarbrough

INK
BRUSH
PRESS

ISBN: 978-0-9883839-5-1
Library of Congress Control Number: 2013930459

Manufactured in the United States

Ink Brush Press
Temple and Dallas

For Sandi, York, Jenni [Chicken], and Sebastian,

Mom and Dad, Don, and Steve

Lee Weldon, Travis, and Slaughter

Rudy, Gloria, Dallie, Peggy, and Matt

Karla, Alan, and Helen Roberts

Poetry from Ink Brush Press

Alan Birkelbach and Karla Morton, *No End of Vision: Texas as Seen by Two Laureates*

Jerry Bradley, *The Importance of Elsewhere*

Millard Dunn, *Places We Could Never Find Alone*

Chris Ellery, *The Big Mosque of Mercy*

Charles Inge, *Brazos View*

Jim McGarrah, *Breakfast at Denny's*

J. Pittman McGehee, *Growing Down*

Carol Coffee Reposa, *Shimmer*

Steven Schroeder, *a dim sum of the day before*

Steven Schroeder and Sou Vai Keng, *a guest giving way like ice melting*

Jan Seale, *The Wonder Is*
     Nape

W.K. Stratton. *Dreaming Sam Peckinpah*

Chuck Taylor, *At the Heart*

Jesse Waters, *Human Resources*

Scott Yarbrough, *A Sort of Adam Infant Dropped: True Myths*

For information on these and other Ink Brush Press books go to
     www.inkbrushpress.com

Acknowledgments

I am grateful to the following journals for publishing my poems.

The American Poetry Review: "This Little Piggy"

Art Times: "Easter Sunrise Service Alone Overlooking the Guadalupe River"

Bellowing Ark: "She Fits Into" and "Regeneration"

Black River Review: "Tiresias"

BlueStem and Illya's Honey: "Vein-Faced Dolls with Eyes"

Concho River Review: "I Want to Die Like Johnny Cash" and "Buzzard Starts

Fire: A Texas Newspaper Headline"

The Cream City Review: "While She is in Michigan"

The Distillery: "Teaching Gilgamesh to College Freshmen"

The Evansville Review: "Ketchup"

The Hollins Critic: "And Those Hands I Never Knew"

The Hurricane Review: "Oedipus Rex Meets Tiresias at Walmart"

Illya's Honey: "Upon contemplating the Tile Floors in Isla Mujeres"

Kit Kat Review: "Family Reunion" and "He Once Asked why I Teach Mythology"

New Texas: "Those Winged Men" and "War Like a River"

Old Hickory Review: "The Restless" and "The Great Cottonwood"

Piedmont Literary Review: "Little Sister's Red Dress at the Wedding"

Pointed Circle: "Playground Rules" and "Your Analyst's Speech He'll Never Give"

Puerto Del Sol: "Halloween: For the Sake of Tradition"

REAL:RE Arts & Letters: "I Respect My Father"

Riversedge: "Four Days Early She Left Laguna Madre" and "Icy Roads at Christmas" "What Stevie Knew and Sandi" and "War Like A River"

Spindrift: "Medusa in Kindergarten" and "Sunday School Lesson"

Windmill: "Role Playing"

Wounded Pulse: "She Said it Might Improve Our Marriage if I Vacuumed"

Zillah: "Protesting Plath" and "Rosa Parks"

CONTENTS

I. Personal Myths

1   This Little Piggy

3   I Respect My Father

4   Ketchup

6   Regeneration

7   A Necktie and a Hijab

8   Easter Sunrise Service Alone Overlooking the Guadalupe River

9   Your Analyst's Speech He'll Never Give

12 Vein-Faced Dolls With Eyes

14 Villanelle for My Friend Who Said I Couldn't Write a Closed Form Poem

15 Up on the Roof

16 Trumpet Vines

18 My Soul Mate Called From Albuquerque

20 Easter Morning on the Comal River: Communion and Sacrifice

23 Halloween: for the Sake of Tradition

25 Upon my Cousin's Decision to Kill Himself

27 The Restless

28 Icy Roads at Christmas

30 Measure for Measure

31 Mama Ree's Funeral

34 She Fits Into

36 Family Reunion

38 Four Days Early She Left Laguna Madre

40 And Those Hands I Never Knew

41 While She is in Michigan

43 Considering the Camberley-Gunter Hotel While the Baby is Asleep

45 Cabbage Rolls

46 Cancer, a Squirrel, My Niece in Love

II. Teaching Universal Myths

51 Invoking the Muse

52 Sunday School Lesson

54 I Want to Die Like Johnny Cash

55 Role Playing

57 Oedipus Rex Meets Tiresias at Walmart

60 Sandy Cheeks, Sponge Bob, and Antigone

62 How to do Laundry

64 Medusa in Kindergarten

66 Memorial Day Poem

66 What Stevie Knew and Sandi

70 Buzzard Starts Fire

72 Playground Rules

74 Teaching *Gilgamesh* to College Freshman

75 His First Nativity

77 Floating the Comal River with Grandpaw

78 Those Winged Men

77 Because I Wrote it Down

80 She Said It Might Improve our Marriage if I Vacuumed

82 The Great Cottonwood

83 Putting "It" in "Its" Place

85 Rosa Parks

86 Tiresias

88 Protesting Plath

89 Didn't Pinocchio Know?

90 Catch and Release

91 War Like a River

92 On a Run I Figure Out U.S./Eastern Relations

94 Little Sister's Red Dress at the Wedding

95 He Once Asked Why I Teach Mythology

97 Be Careful What You Wish For, Little Girl

I. Personal Myths

This Little Piggy

Mother left we three boys in the finned Fairlane,
West Texas windows rolled down, a quick zip into
the Piggly Wiggly for whole milk and Log Cabin syrup.

My oldest brother, Don, noticed the green face of the
dollar bill first on the asphalt waving its corner
like a gift. The middle brother, Steve, came

up with the idea that if each one held one
leg, then they could lower me to retrieve
the prize. They dropped me on my head.

I got the dollar and stood crying by
the door of the car. Don talked Horace Crenshaw
into putting me back through the window

for fifty cents: Horace drank cough medicine
and aftershave; he took the dollar and gave
us back two quarters. Steve said he and

Don would clean the blood off my forehead
for a quarter each so mother wouldn't spank me
when she got back for being bloody for no reason.

All the way home I see myself as a little
cartoon Piggly Wiggly pig wearing
a diaper, my voice stuffed shut with that proverbial

1

red apple, a sort of Adam infant dropped

on asphalt left to noun my new terrain.

This little pig knew then, I was all on my own.

I Respect My Father

I respect my father when he serves communion
to the congregation. He is one of the holy men.
The way he drops the wafers on the extended tongues
and says, "This is the body that died for you;"

the way he cradles the cups of grape juice, sweet;
not what you would think blood would taste like at all;
how smooth the whole operation is, that forgives a whole
congregation in just a few traditional gestures.

It almost seems too easy. That's why
I respect my father, because he never
makes light of the sacrament—even when a child
sneaks a few extra crackers, or slurps

from the Eucharist during the prayer, or rolls his eyes
like Christ on a Catholic cross, or insists
he needs another drink of that sweet blood
to wash that bitter body down.

Ketchup

I work in Vegas: the sidewalk café outside Paris: the one
across from the Bellagio Fountain, the fountains dance
to Andrea Bocelli; his last note always makes my spine
stand and know why God gave man the ability to sing.

When someone orders ketchup with their French Fries
the kitchen buzzes, "Some unrefined idiot."

My father sang when he gardened; he was tone deaf, but
he belted it out between his tomatoes the size of a fist,
just as firm, red as a Coca Cola sign. Sometimes you couldn't
even see him, only his voice, his fingers meticulously picking
those menacing horned green worms, the cat purring,
rubbing her muzzle against the heel of his shoes. Fresh tilled soil.

When I was ten, he parboiled a wheelbarrow full of tomatoes
over a mesquite fire, cooled them in ice water, then peeled
them and pressed them through the sieve, added brown sugar, vinegar,
fresh mustard, 1051 sweet onion, and Allspice. He simmered
it down as he drank a High Life beer pulled straight from the ice water
we peeled the tomatoes in. Then, he had me turn

the potatoes behind the red cedar shed and quarter them.
He fried them in fresh lard, salted them with cracked
pepper and Kosher salt, still singing off key.

"Dip those in that." I did. My spine stood.

When someone orders ketchup and fries, I don't
bring them a saucer with a dollop; I apologize
that I can't bring a wheelbarrow full. I, also, assume
they will not need a glass for their ice cold beer.

Regeneration

Ten hours ago our bare skin was touching
and her mouth was open with her lips against
mine under flannel sheets in an ocean of bed.
Time was balanced between tick and tock.
It is Thursday evening and she is somewhere between
here and never. The air is heavy and sits
under mist and the tires smack against
the wet dew. And it will get colder
and it will get colder. Ice.

One black Grackle blends into night in that
stark tree outside my window. The leaves fall
like cardboard sheets; lights leave their glass houses.
Underneath the earth the tomatoes' sinewy roots loosen;
their toes uncurl; their hair freezes green;
plump red fruit wrinkles inside the cocoon as the seeds
push their way through earth to be born.
Inside you the first cell splits, the miracle set in motion
as Winter holds Spring's small fingers driving eastward.

A Necktie and a Hijab

I wondered how far this woman had traveled to stand
in this grade school lobby in Plano, Texas: Middle-Eastern,
coal-eyed, young mother, Hijab, looking in desperation at
her son, her fingers trembling over an untied American tie.

He was due onstage in several minutes. Her eyes pleaded,
locked with mine—against her culture. I took the tie, stood
behind the boy, turned his collar up. He looked
up, backward at me, smiled upside down.

Fix the length of the short end and around once,
like every time I went to work after school, Piggly Wiggly;
up and through and over back like getting ready for college graduation;
around and through like I did for my son's first recital;

pull tight, down to snug, square the knot like before my daughter's funeral.

I turned him around and showed him his reflection in the trophy
case's glass. He gave me a "thumbs up," the mother's
smile reflected over my shoulder; I moved to hug her.
"It's disrespectful," she whispered to me, "Instead, I will hug

you with my eyes." I, then, realized how far I had
traveled from a West Texas farm town to be hugged
by a woman's eyes in this grade school lobby of Dallas suburbia.
A Necktie and Hijab woven together in one dignified embrace.

Easter Sunrise Service Alone Overlooking the Guadalupe River

The truth sits calmly hidden like a phantom shade
below this air and sky, below that mirrored plane
in a world of fins and gills and eyes that never blink.

While she is in bed now with each twitch and twinkle
and fleck of glitter in defiance of a simple sun that rises
too slowly, I drown in this painting of God; nature

is a nursemaid to heaven, I suppose, praising each morning
and having no argument with consciousness while we become
only what we wish to become in dreams or eternal concoctions.

We all comb our pine needles too straight at times
and at others leave them wide as the drunken grape
that reaches its tipped corners into dark places. Is every morning

this miraculous? Is every challenge this great?
Last night we hurled angry words at each other
Just before our anniversary; there are many bodies

stacked between any relationship. Now there
is no sound other than the pent-up push
of water creasing down the dam's wall, and my faith

is locked in the bottom of this Bloody Mary morning. The birds begin
to chatter wildly and spiral into the sun in search of instinct.
I do not understand this sunrise, this metamorphosis, this cycle.

Your Analyst's Speech He'll Never Give

Simple—it started at church school. You
were both what your parents'
told you not to want. Now between you in bed
are children you didn't plan, a house
mortgage, ennui, and adultery—in that order.
each day the double bed sags with missed
promotions, the way he bites his nails.

He made love to that girl from Abilene exactly
where you lie in bed each night.

You want to slap him intelligent, slap
him so hard his baseball glove falls off,
that his voice drops and matures,
that years of hoarded change clangs to the floor
enough to pay every debt, knocked
silly in love again, trying to get into your pants
all the time again, making the best macaroni
and cheese in the world.

But that's not how it works. For some
reason, God gave us too much memory.

You separate. You keep the house and the girls,
sweethearts, who become two full plates for
the amputated wife to carry and everything in
your life is cut in half or doubles. All while you

never see the moon because it is always just
behind the yellow start. Then, they visit his
Santa Claus house for ten seconds and you become
a crisp cicada cocoon, wondering where your
shiny life crawled off to.

You can never be complete except for small
tastes of ocean and sky; full gives way eventually.

Why couldn't superman-quick-dick father children
with volume knobs, and on/off switches, that
never go pee-pee, with mechanical eyes that close automatically
at eight and sparkling pull-string voices that
say, "Mama" like candied respect. Maybe you
should have shagged the brains out of the exterminator.

You want to laugh until your smile sticks, wrestling
under crisp white sheets where no one ever gains
weight or snores or has nightmares or dies in his sleep.
But it's really pharmaceuticals and the hidden rum
bottle under the bed where you started your period
the first night he left; instead of changing the sheets,
you just slept on his side of the bed.

The sun will rise soon. All this clutter of night will burn
into the clarity of morning. All this absurdity will
reorganize itself and stack itself into perfect compartments. You'll
be Mary Poppins with the children cleaning "spit spot." Maybe the girls
will even develop British accents and jump in and out of chalk
drawings and dance like marionettes on chimney tops.

He's across town, now, at Paradise Apartments with
his mattress, an aluminum lawn chair, one spoon,
one fork, one plate and two magic wands the girls
left behind that he is circling in the dark, trying
so desperately to conjure some incantation
to reverse the wheels of time and temptation.

Vein-Faced Dolls with Eyes

She spoke of what frightened her when she was young.
Those mindless, vein-faced dolls with eyes that won't
close: Halloween. "But," she added, "It was also tricks
and kissing game treats with boys in the alley
just behind my parents' concrete driveway knowing I'd never grow old."

Strange how one random story can swirl back school desks
and black rimmed glasses and hollow pumpkin heads and disguises.

In West Texas, when I was in third grade, a teenager
stopped and dropped a raw egg into my Halloween sack;
a cruel adolescent trick; it soaked, quietly chewed
a hole, then littered my candy out in little trails
from door to door: I ended
with an empty soggy sack. Yesterday,

Regina told me her husband's doctor asked him to remember
three words to test his short term memory. "Baseball,"
she said was the first; she couldn't remember
the other two, because he didn't even remember
the first question: Vascular Dementia. He's going crazy.
She's sure of it: a mindless doll with eyes that won't close.

Did I mention the raw egg
in the Halloween sack in West Texas,
hatching and splitting its horrid plan,
eating away, dotting a trail

with all that free candy falling out
like a spilled genetic code, funneling
memory out of a hollowing skull
like seeds sifted from the belly
of a Jack-O-Lantern?

When she left today, I thought, there's no
easy way home for her now, except to follow
that sweet candy trail over the concrete driveway
past the wrinkled boys, home to her
mindless doll where she'll have to watch an
aging witch fly across her mirror night after night.

Villanelle for My Alcoholic Friend Who Said
I Couldn't Write a Closed Form Poem

At five o'clock the cocktail's crystal clinks
And so the transformation quickly comes
Diluted promises pour down bathroom sinks

Yesterday and day before on golfing links
He told himself, "Just drink on holes with ones"
At five o'clock the cocktail's crystal clinks

Two a.m, one more smoke he thinks
And maybe one last Coke with pool and rum
Diluted promises pour down bathroom sinks

He slyly coaxed to bed a Coke-white mink
Maybe two more lines and then be done
At five o'clock the cocktail's crystal clinks

The children up too early Sponge Bob Inc.
He wakes beside the tub to hide the gun
Diluted promises pour down bathroom sinks

And you, my friend, who cannot find the sun
Begin again and promise truth in fun
At five o'clock the cocktail's crystal clinks
Diluted promises pour down bathroom sinks

Up on the Roof

I returned from getting barbeque sandwiches to find
my wife sitting cross-legged on the roof above the driveway.
Her reason was legitimate: she wanted to see
the hot air balloons float by from the nearby festival.
Then, curiosity had given way; the immigrant
next door was worried she might fall. He had
his son, Antonio, translate. She invited them up;
Sandi, Ignacio, and Antonio cross-legged
on the roof above the driveway. I instantly had the new job
of beer runner and snack patrol. "OK," I'll bite
our neighbor on the other side with the monkey asked—
[This is not a symbolic monkey; my neighbor has a monkey.]
By my next trip out with Coronas, they wanted music.
I put Dave Brubeck on the portable turntable I found
in the closet; I thought it rather approachable for
everyone, even the monkey. During "Far More Blue,"
there was the first balloon as big as a Zeppelin growing over the trees.
The son pointed and the father machine gunned a phrase.
The son rushed and returned with Margarita, the wife;
she pulled herself up the makeshift ladder; Ignacio
pushed her butt and Antonio pulled and the monkey moved over.
"She's never seen a balloon that people ride in," Antonio explained.

A flash of color over and over, balls of color and shapes rising
in the sun while breathy reeds and wire brushes on snares
circled above us delivering dreams somewhere over the trees
touching the floor of heaven, stirring consciousness
somewhere between primate, man, and God.

Trumpet Vines

The cold morning snap surprised
the trumpet vine's blooms. They fell.
My sister placed one orange flame
on each finger and pretended
to be a witch. Dad
whistled. We jumped in the bed
of the truck. We were late for school.
The engine shuddered, the fan screamed, stopped.

The recent litter of kittens had sought
the warmth of the engine compartment. None
of the four survived. We were taught
not to cry in the driveway. My sister
cried in the driveway. I cried in the closet
while I got a shoe box
to bury them in. At school, I pictured
them all day locked in that dark box,
all crowded together like back
in their mother's belly, safe.
When I got home, I dug
out the flower bed and buried each one,
careful to leave their front paws
out resting, reaching across the fresh soil.
My sister put the trumpet blossoms back
on her fingers and touched
each of the paws with an incantation.
Mother cat watched from the Azalea bush,

curious, she brushed against my sister
who rubbed her with the tips of her trumpet fingers.

The new litter pawed their souls from the earth
into the mother's belly then spilled out
four months later with bodies; their trumpeting
mews calling for mother's milk and Spring.

My Soul Mate Called From Albuquerque
For Sigrid

My soul mate called and told me she was dying
under her husband's heavy weight.
We grew up the broken children of our own god,
a Phoenix meeting itself in each morning's fire.

We are all dead,
and born again each morning.

Across the city a lover lies snoring and fat,
after empty cans and pretty
pills to balance the light and dark on his nose,
but she'll carry the weight of those seconds for nine
heavy months.

My cat made love to six cats
on the porch four moons ago while the
children watched and laughed at their
howling:
the mother died
giving birth on York's bed. An hour later
I pulled the nursing kittens
off her empty breasts.

How many gardens of squash and yellow corn
and firm red tomatoes must I push
into the dark earth to watch
rust under winter's heavy skirt?

Don't talk to me of night's dark tunnel;
all I can remember is your smile:
slow and dry, and your laugh,
how you fed me
like biting into an orange,

rind and all,
ripe and tart,
sunshine and smile,
sweet sinewy pulp and peel.

Easter Morning on the Comal River: Communion and Sacrifice

Mother invited her boys for Easter to the Comal River.
"Poets and thought make no money. Business
law is a good profession," she greeted me,
handing me my fruit basket—tradition.
I squeezed her welcome into a screwdriver—tradition.
The world revolves around whatever
egocentric location I'm in.

I love my parents; they just don't know
I'm the same age they were when mother
bought their cemetery plots. "Let's go
fishing," my oldest brother, Don, rescues me
and my middle brother, Steve.

Outside, the sun rises in a rhythm; my heart beats
blood in blue rivers just under my skin.

I wonder if the dragonfly puzzling over
the fishing line is concerned with his mother's
affirmation. The river floats
as it must to the sea. Trees spin
their roots into the puzzled bank, and water
simply twists into the weak spot, prying
bark and pulls it gently away. The pill
bug works through the stiffest
carcass erasing identity to dust.

There are those on earth whose job it is to homogenize.

Nature is a wave that overtakes herself; she answers
her own questions. She wakes
and never sleeps, evolves
without close supervision—just basic
rules while offering parallels:
my brother and I are fish. Fish are all
brothers living in their glass world. Their
equator is the horrible parallel; if
they break, they would have to wear some silly
awkward breathing device. My mother is
the horrible oxygen that we need watered down. My father the hard-
headed snail, one-footed monosyllabic determination.
The grandchildren are the birds testing
their voices against the rising sun
circling incessantly toward instinct.

Sunrise is its own miracle; it raises the dead;
fish are even known to top the water in expanding circles.

"Mother wanted us back by ten," Don says.
the bell tower two blocks over mouths
out the ending hour. "The Train
is coming." We press our sides against the rail
of the bridge. I feel the earth clench. "Hold
onto the rail. The train knows
where it is going," Steve teases me. The bass flips
one last time in the creel.

Let the rising sun wear down
the squirrels to forage: that's their duty,
not frolicking. "Drinking is a *noble* profession,"
I sneer a toast but my drink
is empty and the cornucopia
has become a drunkard's mouthpiece.

Mother's heavy feet shuffle through the kitchen
towards strait slices of marbled bacon, his body,
and tomato juice, his blood, to dissect
my marbled profession over communion and
sacrifice because they are the sustenance of life.
Poet's and thought are not. Don lifts his asthma
mask and secures it over his ears and Steve
laughs at the spray, click, breathe, spray,
click, breathe pretending he is drowning.

Halloween: for the Sake of Tradition

We seek the forbidden because it is delicious:
Eve's apple; Niobe's tear; she searching
for him without a name or face.
Outside the lonely cats meow
on the stoops half-tamed against
the wilderness, consoled by our children.

Last night York and Jenni carved
the pumpkin while she ran away
from me. They carved the grim
faces, trimmed the melon teeth
and pulled the guts—seeds and orange meal—
from the belly of the head
and lowered a careful candle
in to light the hollow eyes,
while she looked for him.

She needs to know again.
I need to know again, too.
After I turned thirty, it was
as if I were intoxicated, cursed
with some horrible secret, standing
alone in a crowd of sober people.

Why did our fathers and mothers never tell us?
Why did they throw their words
behind closed bedroom doors?

Yesterday she told me she
hated the way I rub my nose.
It's come to that.

Tonight I'll bed my jealousy.
But before I can stop, I'll have said too much,
wrapped up our own condition,
thrown open Pandora's cedar box,
but all for the sake of tradition.

Upon My Cousin's Decision To Kill Himself

He used a German Lugar his father toted
back from WWII. Imagine what that gun
had to do to get back to Abilene, Willis Street.
It could have just as easily rusted under sand
on Omaha beach, but someone decided
it needed to float an ocean. He shot himself in the chest.

Suicide is a secret that is just about to spill and color
the earth a color besides blood red. Blood is easier.

He was left-handed, so he would have had
to hold the barrel with his right
just away from his chest and pull
the trigger with the thumb and index of his left
hand, like a looking glass searching for a purpose.

I mean, suppose the calculation. Suppose
he would have hung himself: cutting the rope;
is it strong enough; which tree; how far
should I fall before it catches; the measuring
tape; looking up "Hangman's Noose."
                                 That might
be where he saw a picture of the human heart,
in the "H's," and how it's just to the left of center
like he was.
               Then, he must have considered
how that indifferent bullet with hollow head

would spread and push its way into his heart
like an instant cancer, indifferent.

Suicide is everything that leads up to it. But ultimately
it is that second when one jumps or pulls or thinks
the world is better off without them. None are right.

We needed him suffering or not.

At the family reunion I'll have to make my own Colorado Bulldogs
and try to remember his megaphone laugh and his Texas
running shorts pulled up so high we had to turn our eyes.

What was so bad that a bottle
of wine and key lime pie couldn't cure?
I really wish he wouldn't have done that.

The Restless

My daughter walks in her sleep, five years
old and already troubled, in her pink pajamas
with rubber-soled feet. A marionette dropped
hard from the heavens: marble-eyed,
pink-cheeked and numb, moving recklessly
through night's dark tunnel.

Perhaps she's eating candy mountains,
or all of her dolls are alive
and dancing with her, armless, balancing
on one leg, painted
with red lipstick and rouge.

By morning she'll be exhausted
droopy-eyed, popsicle-stick legs
under an iron-bell dress, feelings
on a white starched sleeve,
runny nose and milk moustache.

I'll never know what secrets she has
hidden behind those wandering planets.

Icy Roads at Christmas

On Christmas Eve, my father drove
in tense posture, elbows flared
under the frozen lights dripping
their crystal bellies in fat clean drops:
cherry, lemon, grape, and green.

That's what I remember.

My father's late, stumbling body beneath the neon sky.
Obediently, I stood with the men, boots
churning the soil with snow, opening my palms
to be read by the butane heater that hissed
its blue tongue into the night like a beacon.

The smell of liquor and laughter ascended across time
through their coarse valleys, those howling Wise men,
directing my father to his own immaculate death.

At first it was just a heaviness in his chest that he ignored:
dodging headlights, mindlessly waving to the children hanging
from the Ford pickup window. He finally fell lifeless beside
the sad cat's meow that twisted around his feet
like a small tornado. He never even saw

that red neon cross he upset
that fell and cracked
that bled against the earth like the brittle hope of Easter.

Christmas Eve has always been a problem for me.
Santa died in 1969, in Weslaco. After his funeral
grandmother Yarbrough borrowed a blender from Ben Franklin's
in her black Sunday dress and made fresh Ruby Red Daiquiris;
that Christmas was a taste of honey that crawled
from the back of the tongue to the tip
and reposed between the lips of the night
like a sad Magnolia leaf, southern with a drawl,
white and curling like the loins of a secret
too heavy to be hoisted. Just eight, I slept drunk
in her snoring arms all night.

Christmas Day has always been a shrill voice, startling,
calling my name like a mother, beating
a great oatmeal pan, throwing
her yellow hair in the doorway.
It's tedious, really, hard to rise
to the occasion. Santa and Jesus
have always been the same person to me, really.

Measure for Measure: Considering the Tile Floor at Two O'clock AM in Isla Mujeres

The tiles rule the room in rigid squares,
But those who enter never know they're measured
The grout counts the tiles, nothing spare.

A secret couple carefully avoids the stairs.
Then flail their flesh and sinuous passion treasured.
The tiles rule the room in rigid squares.

Orange striped, the cat sleeked the stairs
to arch then sleep across the moment squared.
The grout counts the tiles, nothing spare.

The drunk who fists, rages all life's snares,
puts to bed his deathly woes westward.
The tiles rule the room in rigid squares.

The maid, bleached mop, morning eating pears,
beats the white head, waking all the bedded.
The grout counts the tiles and nothing spare.

And here, myself, with sleeping wife, half bare:
She's the grout, my soul, my bones, my treasure.
The tiles rule the room in rigid squares.
The grout counts the tiles and nothing spare.

Mama Ree's Funeral

Grandma would much rather have dropped
dead of a simple life
in the apple orchard between the two
Appaloosa horses, or even been eaten
by a Brown Bear while checking
the water level in the cistern, but nature plays
those tricks of asking what you want—

                              then giving converse.

Cancer ultimately kills its host.
It ridiculously feeds a selfish
ego that supposes it might just cheat
death to become the living body. It reads
its maps and splits and blooms
too quickly, too big, too pretty
for a sordid adolescence it can't outlive. In reality,
its death is just as untimely and tragic
as the victim it slowly fills.

That's how we get to the Funeral.

It was a good, routine New
Mexico foothills funeral: nasal singing,
too small of church, and a good
eulogy. Then the absurd set in as
it always must. There's only so much
we can plan: the opening
of the casket at the end heebeegeebeed

me; anything that makes a room-full

of cowboys and war vets squirm

is questionable. And to boot, since Grandma was dying

of cancer, she was allowed the convenience

of picking her own "I'm wearing

it forever" dress. She had ultimately dressed

herself for the funeral, gone down

to JoNell's Cosmetics, and then slid

herself into the coffin for a nap. The mortician

never should have closed

the coffin while members of the family

were still viewing. Her body

was elevated to look 'natural'

for viewing and thus

she had to be shoved

down by the shoulders

so that the lid of the coffin closed

wouldn't bend just the tip of Grandma's nose for eternity;

it's a mortician's measure of space. Then,

they locked the coffin. Twice. I suppose

they were afraid she might just slip

out the bottom half and run

crazily into the darkened woods forcing

Persephone to restart the seasons

and humanity to have to wipe

all the calendars clean to start

the Copian converts time table miracle.

"No resurrections please." Begin

the black car bright light parade to the burial.

Grandmother "Darling" [the daughter's wife's mother)
was late to the funeral. She missed
the service and barely
made the graveside. Through her handkerchief, she asked
me to jump down to open the coffin. I told
her, "No. That's ridiculous."
She made me swear "Ree" looked
pretty; I did, because she was. Back

at the church we ate covered dish: Fried Chicken
with double batter, baked Yellow Squash dotted
with black peppercorn and butter, Collard
Greens with pepper hot vinegar,
Coconut Pie just crisp with vanilla on the top, apple
cobbler from Mama Ree's orchard of special Wine-Sap
Sour Apples, Pot roast from the neighbor's slaughter
of "Chalupa: the Cow," chicken enchiladas made
from "Winston," the fighting cock, Mama Ree's favorite Rooster.
He was a pretty shitty enchilada but the Hatch Anaheim chilies
made up for it and seconds and thirds and
what would it have mattered in the scheme of things if I had opened it?

She Fits Into

She fits into those panties
by the television, flesh
under silk that
green bra by the couch
shirt and shoes by the window in the kitchen
by the spilled basil and half squeezed
tomatoes and the water now boiling waiting
for the dry noodles and our beers half empty
gathering beads of sweat on the silver and
on her eyebrows
they can wait but we
my pants halfway down
up the stairs she stops and winks
she kept her socks on.

She kissed my lips later through the sunflowers
and the clear of the shower
curtain while I watched
and she got soap in her mouth
and laughed and she said I tricked
her. I did. I tricked her
into believing in more
than long days that grind
like a boulder on corn
stone and meal
simple pleasure
and later, after I was asleep, she tied

mistletoe above the bed for morning and wrapped
her slumbering limbs around mine like fresh green roots.

Family Reunion

Aunt Gusland retorts after a bite of Cheerios,
"Well, Grandmother Davis was hidden in a whiskey barrel
when she was a baby so the Injuns wouldn't get her."
Mother one-ups her with a piece of bacon,
"Uncle Gilbert—rest his soul—was eaten by wild pigs."
Everyone says, "Poor, poor Gilbert," in unison.

I always picture grandmother as a sort of a midget, fully aware,
her arthritis already curling her hands, her standing rigid
in a dark whiskey barrel. I see the Hollywood
Indians slinging tomahawks, riding underneath
bareback painted Pinto ponies without saddles, aiming arrows
under horses bellies upside down, wearing war paint like crayons;
their skin, sprayed-on orange. The cowboys
are filmed in black and white—for contrast—and
the wagon team driver gets shot. He grimaces
downstage-right into the camera as he half-falls away
upstage: his back bleeds black blood.

Uncle Gilbert? I picture him whistling, pouring a pail
of slop to the happy-go-lucky pigs,
grunting happy grunt songs—when, suddenly,
the music starts: just a bit bothersome at first, then louder
into minor chords against shrill high strings. The pigs start
moving in unison towards some preplanned pig break. One muzzles
up behind Gilbert's canvas pants; the others push
forward. The music becomes feverish as the body

drops, disappears, (horrid screams)—and it's a
Piranha pig feeding frenzy. They back-up in a circle.
Uncle Gilbert is stripped of all skin and sinewy muscle leaving
only the skeleton and his big, left, bug glass-eye, popped
from his skull, and his real eye like sewing thread dangling a ball.

The pigs eye the eyes, confused between what's
real and what seems; they stop mid-grunt.

That's the one quick quip of a person's entire lifetime,
one event, Nixon or Clinton: a great Cottonwood
whittled down to one toothpick.

Are we are all fated to spend eternity in one looped
moment, a stuck phonograph record turning
and turning and turning on our least favorable note?

Four Days Early She Left Laguna Madre

The moon is a simple round hole in the night
tunneling somewhere light, while the waves curl
and curl and throw their able white heads
against the sand looking for the answer.

She sits in her orchid nightie,
her bare thighs almost the same color,
turning the turning the sheets of morning news
reading only the headlines and the obituaries
looking for her dead life.

But the waves, how can they settle their arguments
with just a crash and a run
and that final desperate reach
held in line by the earth?

The moon is a hole tunneling somewhere light,
somewhere away, over hollow fish where the sea is
more than rough shore, ripe
with life, a mothering machine, pumping
creatures from her hidden womb like sparkling gifts.

Death has a darker tongue than all our bickering.

Four days early she left Laguna Madre
her hard life rolled out like a thin tin sheet,
sitting postured, her vodka and juice on the tray,

finishing her survey in *Mademoiselle*,
while the full moon just out her window
balanced on the tip of her wing, tunneled
away somewhere simple, somewhere light,
a hole in the night strong enough to lift
even the sea's tangled troubles.

"They'd of been a good couple if
they just hadn't had to live together,"
Uncle Bill said at the reunion dinner, hands resting
on his belly after the lobster and white wine,
cigar stuffed in his mouth like a brown leather shoe.

And Those Hands I Never Knew

For Estelle Davis

And those hands across our backs are like stones,
heavy confirming pats. "She was old enough to die,"
Flora Crenshaw said from her bed as she dropped
her teeth coldly into the plastic cup on her nightstand.

For ten years in the nursing home, her body bitterly
bowed and curled under each day's added heaviness. Her
fingernails perused her palms looking for her lost life.
Her knees curled and lifted to touch her dried breasts.

She didn't die like he did ten years ago. Men then were
silent dunes moving under the blue sky towards something. She
slowly consumed herself like a snake swallowing her own tail.
Grandmother moved cautiously toward death. She sensed the

nothing. That's why she stayed alive. The night she died, she
told me there were crowded corners of herself she did not know.
Two minutes later she told me there were seventy-two ducks
glued to the wallpaper on her west wall. I never knew.

While She Is In Michigan

Tonight the air is thin;
she has spent her water down.
The secret sits trapped
in the red gills of a carp
feeding beside the shore
on knuckles of yellow corn.

Time seems to stand like an
old woman now, bending.
She used to flow over green moss,
rich and hungry,
in sheets across the plains
to salty bottomless pools.

While she is in Michigan, here
the elms curl their green
fingers to the soil, thumping the ground
like dry rain.
This grey year,
The snow dusted sleeping cats in Texas
while she waited patiently by the lake.
Here it is already winter,
and already I dream of browned flesh
oiled and almost naked in the sun.

But we can't rush the seasons;
we must calculate them:

extend our sleeves,

turn up our collars,

and hide our heads from the cold,

like ancient turtles growing old.

Considering the Camberley-Gunter Hotel While Blaine (The Baby) is Asleep

Somewhere in the corner darkness
of the architect's mind something popped
bright, a crystal thought of structure. Imagine
the first push of the shovel that swelled
then hollowed the soil. Watch as steely
ribs spread heavenward from earthly site
beside copper veins water-filled. The stones turn
and stack and fit like a puzzled-prophecy
with cement coat. It stretches and yawns
and rises floor by floor, awakening
to babble its confounded
tongue at the sky.

We will always coronate
the earth with her own entrails, turn
her inside out,
heave her upon herself. Certainly,

like the aging architect, this building must also
tire. After nagging the heavens, after rain licks
at her feet and uninvitingly looks under her doors
into her sinew, she must tire, too.
We can stuff facelifts into her wrinkling
facade. We can council her after storms
and paint her seasoned insides white again;
but still the grout crumbles in the shower's

corner; her putty lines sag; her carpet
tastes shoe after shoe. She will finally fall.
We are all mortal.

But the baby is crying to announce
her awakening. Everything
is new to each new generation; we cannot
pass on certain experiential knowledge. In the shifting
sands of the desert eventually those pyramids will quietly
repose and the Sphinx will lose his nose. Even
that god on such strong thighs will return to each
grain of sand before he was mined from Gaea's
core to celebrate our ever-fading ornament.

But the baby is crying louder now.
Even her seeds from mothers past
are crying forward with perpetual promise inside.

Cabbage Rolls

"Stay behind this cabbage truck. Don't pass,"
my grandmother told my brother. We were hungry,
ready to be home from crossing into Mexico. The Rio
Grande Valley is a pregnant mother earth,
pushing forth Ruby Red Grapefruit, plump
with spraying juice, 1015 Sweet
Onions the size of softballs. Out our windshield
cabbage was stacked like a bed full of sleepy heads,
riding the wooden rails of the transport truck.
"Wait for the railroad track." The truck rattled
over the track. Five cabbages peeked up and over,
fell to the asphalt, rolling into an onion field. "Stop.
You little ones go get those and pull an onion." We did.

That night we ate boiled cabbage with salt pork fat,
1015 Onion fresh, cabbage squeaking against our teeth.

Grandmother knew cabbage would fill our young
bellies up enough to sleep, even without meat;
we went to bed faux full, content watching my Chickasaw
grandmother exercising her instinct:

the practice and patience to follow the food,
to know where crossroads lie, and to gather
her pack content with action not words.

Cancer, a Squirrel, My Neice in Love

"I never thought raising a teenage daughter
would be more difficult than cancer treatment."
The text was from my sister-in-law. Don't text
and drive. I looked up, tried to veer. The squirrel,
start-stopped in that comic book pose. He went
under the back right tire. I stopped with a steering-wheel,
two-palmed, "Dammit." His tail shook
like a surrender flag; the girl squirrel
sat behind the Oak tree, peeking out: mating season.

I got out, picked the squirrel up by his tail.
My mother's voice called, "Touching dead
animals will give you a disease." That made
me hold him to my heart harder, blood
on my shirt trying to reunite him with himself.
Cancer, squirrel, my niece in love.

He's not dirty; he's my mother's fear of the unknown.

Blaine, sixteen, my niece, her grades have dropped
in spite of being brilliant and talented. Like a squirrel
in heat, she's a growl and a puff around Spencer, her boyfriend.
Her mother knows that sound; that sound made her child.

Her father knows that sound. It's the same one that made
his child; Blaine had only purred until this point. They've
never heard the guttural longing of their daughter

who understands them now, except in the embers
of their coal fire brains and red hearts they've hung
loosely in the licorice closet on bended hangers.

We fear what we have survived.
Youth consumes a product all at once.

Lori's cancer is playing hide-and-seek in its infancy, being a
reclusive, entitled bitch, and I don't want it to find
puberty. I want it to die a comet flying into the sun,
so I can have her lecture me about tomatoes and soccer and
how hard her grandchildren are to worry about while holding
hands with her stoic husband who made it across the street.

II. Teaching Universal Myths

Invoking the Muse

She is the cornucopia spilling pomegranates
into nests. She cradles my journey to unknown
garden to harvest her grain and brew my liquor.

She is my shield, my cloak and courage, veiling
me, pulling me from safe home and gate
to cliff and cave and finally darkness' grave.

There, her womb digests me into breath,
wisdom to word to call out the mouthpiece
of her mother loss. She bears me forward

from cradle to coffin and fresh full moon
sliced to feed insatiable flesh made word.
She sings through me her soul, my word, our song.

Sunday School Lesson

Jesus is grape juice and crackers to me.
My brothers and I were such a handful
we were banned from our father's house
on Sunday. Dad was the preacher. Instead

our mother made us ring the bells
from the barn next door at straight
up noon. We were small so the bells
pulled my brothers off the floor.

"I'm going to heaven,' Steve would say
the big bell lifting him. Don said, "And back
down to this cow floor of manure." I
always reached for Steve's legs just in case

he saw the tips of God's toes. Once,
during sermon we snuck into
the church and ascended the back staircase
to explore the third floor closet;

We found the trap door to the steeple
and looked at the moon full in the middle
of the day; Dad did that. Mother made
him do it just to show us skipping sermon

made the moon shine in the middle of the day.
She told us God was doing extra God stuff

for us that he really didn't have the time for while
Africans were starving and Indians were dotting their heads.

I repented by finishing off the leftover Communion,
a half a loaf of unleavened bread and forty-six
shots of Jesus' blood. That afternoon, mother spanked me
for throwing up Jesus just behind the third pew.

My father forgave me.

I Want to Die Like Johnny Cash

I want to die like Johnny Cash,
black eyes riveted just past destiny.
I want to lean on darkness like a friend.
I want a woman, long black hair, big bright soul
to sit behind me with those "he's everything," eyes.
I want Willie and dead Waylon and missing Kristofferson
to wail me an "I'm on my way somewhere," highway song.
I want some solitude and distance and a cantankerous velvet
voice you can only get from spending time in your own prison.
I want to sit at the banquet table with death as my uninvited guest,
knowing something must die for me to live.
                                                    So, open the wine
and pour it deeply. Tell death to get comfortable
because I'm not going until I've finished my body and blood because
I am going to die like Johnny Cash.

Role Playing

"What does any of this have to do with that?"
Lauren asked, pointing outside the second
story lecture window above those red
fiery leaves, yellow-tongued. I shifted,
leaving Oedipus dangling between the messenger
and the shepherd, the truth blazing six lines away.

I tried to explain carefully, "I am
not just curious of your winding intellect
inside your skull or your White-Out addiction."
"Your assignment," I paused, "Is to die
with no coins in the ear of your white
pocket, with a raw body still blue-bruised because
you have bedded life like an insatiable lover. If you die
with your arthritic fingers perusing your palms
for obvious creases never taken, you get an 'F.'
However, if you die half-painted, young,
middle-aged, or old, with a mouthful of air rushing
into your crisp gills, blood racing
to the tips of your unfolding limbs, you get an 'A.'"
No one said a word. "Where does light
go when it leaves its glass house?" I asked
and exited as always: first to my office,
then spiraling down the staircase, past Information,
under the fishbowl window of the academic Dean,
through the exit, spilling into the absurd world.

It is all a routine.

At my car, I find a red

lipstick kiss on my windshield,

and a note under the wiper's blade.

It read, "Thank you for yelling," signed, "Lauren."

And it is I who am reminded, in a single

gesture infinitely more powerful

than my lifetime of meticulously gathered rhetoric,

that this journey is Pass/Fail,

and that grades can be turned in anytime.

Oedipus Rex Meets Tiresias at Walmart

I can never find a parking spot by the door. What
I wouldn't give to be handicapped sometime. Get
one of those wheelchair stickers, which, by the way, a clubfoot
doesn't quality. I could kill that guy in the Hummer who cut me
off, like he's manager or something. Damn Walmart.

I'm here to return my wife's, "Do it Yourself: Family Tree"
PC disk, in trade for a pair of toga brooches. How
do you wear out a brooch? Stick it "again" and "again"
and "again?" Honestly, sometimes she treats me like a boy; her
little Ashton. That was mean. Still, Creon, her
worthless brother, just sits around on his ass all day.

"Have a return?" Name tag: Tiresias. There's one
for the baby names book. "Just a disk; not opened."
"Sure you don't want to take a look at that?"
His blind person stick nudges my foot like a hint.
I hate interrogations. "Well, have a smiley
face sticker and give my regards to your family."
I put the sticker in my pocket so Ismene can
have it when I get home. "Could I get one
more; Antigone will just hang herself if Ismene
gets one and she doesn't. Just like her mother."

I find the woman's accessories aisle—Togas, laurels,
choreographing chorus cards, herbs for alters,
wrinkle cream, drapes, Sphinx repellent—then, there

they are, solid silver with zirconium heads, brooches perfect
enough for a queen. Women don't ever know what we
go through to please them, such a riddle.

I check out with just a chorus of people all bitchin'
about how horrible the country's immigration policy is
and the drought. 'This exchange
is going to be tragic,' I think to myself; then,
almost like fate; I get some older displaced
Cesar Chavez farm worker who used to do
odd jobs for me on the mountain behind the house
and he recognizes me, really knows his stuff. Seems
like he was in an awful hurry though; no real time to chit-chat.

I pass the glasses shop on my way to the door
and remind myself to get an eye exam, *soon*.
"Be sure and keep that receipt," Tiresias smiles a
cookie-dough wrapped around obesity smile.
Where do they get these people anyway? I hold
up my bag, like a secret, like they want you to,
like you found the meaning of life at Walmart.

I notice the sun falling over the red western sky,
a candy sundrop fame flashing gone. How much
time have I wasted on this one errand in the wilderness?

"You might need to return something," he adds.
"You might need to return something," I say sarcastically
under my breath. What a know-it-all. And to think all
I have to look forward to at home is whether or not

the two boys have settled their argument yet. I might
as well blindly wish my life away to retirement in
the white clouds and calm of Colonus.

Sandy Cheeks, Sponge Bob, and Antigone

During lecture, I can see out the window;
The students can't. Today, a dog has found
a plastic, see-through, Sam's-sized canister
of Cheeto balls with two meshed inseparably,
sugared with the last of a Coke and a sticky
Jolly Rancher, apple, I would guess.

Antigone defying Creon, the dog
managed to get her head stuffed like a pimento
into the clear, plastic olive. After
lapping up the Cheetos, she found her head stuck.
For minutes she spun around; Antigone
said she had heard Creon's decree. Then, she galloped;
Ismene reminded Creon that Haemon was betrothed
to Antigone. Then, in desperation, she wagged her head
like growling a towel; Antigone tells the Chorus
she'd rather not have to die to be a martyr.
Exhausted, the dog finally lay resigned to imprisonment,
head in a plastic globe, beginning to fog over
from her wet breath, the heat turning her soul fluid.

Antigone hanged herself; Haemon spat on his father and killed
himself rather half-to-the-hilt and Creon's wife, Eurydice,
pretty fed up with it all, leaned on a knife at the alter.

I dismissed class; a boy at the back stood
and immediately felt the authority to noun the mutt's predicament.

"Look! Sandy Cheeks on Sponge Bob."

They all laughed and pointed and swam outside

and soaped Sandy's neck and set her free

to conquer land problems. Then, they dispersed, a conquering

group of Sponge Bob's and Patrick's,

infant-gilled freshmen, to solve

the dark problems of the sea where

cartoon sponges and starfish and girl squirrels

can live in harmony and pester my Squigward muse

to parallel the workings of Thebes and Bikini Bottom.

How to do Laundry: for my Brother-in-law
who Just Moved into an Apartment

Your mother's not here. So get your clothes
and put them in a pile. All of them. That includes
your sheets and underwear. Separate them
into mostly white and mostly color. Then, call your mother

and ask her how she got the blood out
of those white corduroy pants in first grade
when you finally stood up to Roger and pushed
him off the top of the red slide, or the sweat
in those sheets from six days with Chicken Pox
and the pink Calamine lotion she rubbed on every raised red dot.

Next, get all the quarters you were going to spend
on beer. Look in the couch, in the cracks
of the car seat. Look where you hide money;
everyone hides money. Then, call your mother

back and ask her what that detergent was that smelled
like South Padre Island in July and sheets
soft against sunburned skin dried on the clothesline.

Go to the laundromat and act like
you go there all the time; be sure "to stay
while the clothes are in the dryer or the Mexicans
will steal them while you're gone, especially your
underwear." [That's what you think]. Then, call your mother

and ask her how to say, "Thank You" and "Yes, ma'am"
in Spanish because everyone there just wants to help.
They are not there to cut your throat or steal your kidneys.

Throw all your clean clothes in a basket. Fold them
at the laundromat. It's easier there, your mother says,
fold them like you always said she did and take
them home to let them find their clean corners in drawers
and houses on hangers. Then, call your mother

and tell her "Thank You" for still doing your laundry.

Medusa in Kindergarten

Everything was fine until Kindergarten pictures.
Mother had pretty much hijabed me up until that time:
towels tight against their writhing heads; they were silk thin.
Still, they understood like I did. We didn't want attention.

Until, Billy Kosta ripped my scarf in recess one day. I think he
was just curious, and so was I, and they were, too. Alexa—and yes,
they are all named—peeked and caught a corner of Billy's bright glance.
Billy's blue eyes locked up and he was stupid for the rest of his life.

I promised to keep my girls at bay after, but at night during showers
they were always crazy writhing trying to get somewhere,
but they were connected to me. They would tell me to sleep
or to stay awake or to do and do and would never shut up: a head full.

He didn't even know what he was up against. I was not in a good
mood that day when Perseus stepped in. I was in my adolescent aloneness
with those bitchin' girls. And he *needed* a *favor*. I had put a lot of stone
that week, keeping my sisters' place safe, but, I think, I saw in his approach

reflected in that shield, real love, which is really all I ever wanted, frankly.

I always thought it was about me; that somehow I was the heroine.
He gets it though. I don't. I am the snake-headed, green-eyed tragedy.
He gets to be the hero who twisted the witch. I am not a witch. I just
have snakes on my head that tell me to do stuff, and I can't

64

help it if my eyes turn men to stone. Still, I do know

one thing; I always see that look just before they freeze

like they want to crawl inside me and sleep inside my fleshy walls.

Instead, they freeze forever; I suppose I get some pleasure in that.

Memorial Day Poem

We have to earn the right to write poems like this.
Once a year on Memorial Day, I wake just before dawn
and leave her naked long limbs and fresh flesh
under crisp white sheets. She knows and confirms
with a pat that she'll be there when I get back;
I love her and she loves me and we both know it.

I am in my restored El Camino, windows down,
a slow ride with a stiff rum and cranberry and one vicodin
and Dave Brubeck to the market for eggs, a ham steak,
biscuits, heavy cream, coffee, and real butter. Then, back
to cook and then to the backyard to write my Memorial Day poem.
I don't know if I'll write about Iraq or not; that war makes me weary.

The birds spin into morning with first light sparking their coil;
they spin their instinct into the sun singing their
forever song. I like now. I like the smell of now. I wonder how dad felt
leaving young mom naked in bed to put his boots on Omaha beach?
Did the gulls caw their morning instinct that sunrise? Dad once told me,
in confidence, that he drank red wine from a French woman's slipper.

I picture him as some confident John Wayne, modern-day monster
killer, big enough to make Hercules' young battle
look like a boy wrangling with worms. That was their war—boys
against boys and good guys and bad guys, flags against swastikas; the Iraq

war is messy and on TV and melts the skin of children and rapes coal-eyed women
with no sure enemy or way to win and you can't sip wine from sandals.

I walk to the river behind the house; it flows as it must
to the sea and salty bottomless floors. By my foot the
pill bugs are busily working through the stiff carcass
of a squirrel erasing his identity to dust and food for flowers.
There are those on earth whose job it is to homogenize. I suppose
war is a pill bug that digests humanity, returning dust to dust.

Now, I am the bird testing my voice against the rising sun, circling
incessantly toward instinctive extinction like Icarus thumped out of the sky.
We are destruction balanced by naked warm waiting women and confirming pats
and red wine in slippers and early morning cocktails and rivers
that flow to an ocean whose heart never stops beating on the shore
and a simple breakfast with real butter and back to sleep peace eternal.

What Stevie Knew and Sandi

There's a fix that's perfect after dark, music
that feeds the earth and rolls like Stevie Ray's blues.
And Sandi is the moon that sits calm and patient
shining like Halloween candy in the black night.

I told her, "Trouble is always drowned by rain, eventually."
Stevie knew that, spinning his soul like a web
in the open sky, catching note after note in a form
that seemed a musical puzzle until he finished, long

fingers plowing the maple neck of Lenny.
Sandi has those fingers. You should see them.
Stevie died on my birthday and Sandi, fresh as the morning, put
on Texas Flood, and drank a lime daiquiri watching me remember.

Our curse is thought, no doubt. And our destiny is only a taste
of God and of ocean and sky and should never be reduced
to theology or premise. That, I know.
It's sad that any of us have to die; we are all we have.

I know Sandi is precious with her gifts as simple and deep
as a thoughtful stroke of watercolor, a red wash cut
by shadow blue and purple. Like Dionysus, Sandi was
born of fire and carefully hidden, sewn up and stitched tight

in Mercury's thigh, hidden from her own youth by wicked desire. But
She, like the vine, is resilient and finds water each Spring.

I feel simply nothing when she first leaves
Just as I felt when Rudy told me Stevie died.

When Sandi leaves, her fingers hold
so much tenderness, grace, awkward pleasure,
her hair pulled back when she kisses, her keys dangling
in a heap behind my head like a heavy burden, some

clinking a memory, some sagging heavily with forgotten purpose,
beautifully and clumsily she stumbles into each new moment
fresh and open as her brown skin and smile,
her mind moving in shifting patterns toward some distant goal.

Stevie knew something that Sandi knows, too, I think.
Only a few know, really what it is to die:
those who have tasted it; that's why their souls are so tangled,
yellow and bright blue as a bruise; so few challenge the sun.

Buzzard Starts Fire: Texas Newspaper Headline

I imagine him some delinquent adolescent buzzard,
misunderstood, with some arsenal of box matches
on a mission, wearing a placard, "Buzzards
are people, too," flying his mission: lofty,
prideful, strong, vengeful, determined to set
a fire at any suicidal cost, to burn Texas
down to its cowboy boots and rusty spurs.

The summer has been hot here in Dallas,
record heat, the soil is cracked the size
of black Texas Ranger baseball bats: drought. The sad
scientific reality is that the black bird of the animal
kingdom—not by choice, but by genetic code—
simply crawled up the hot sky to try to sit
in the slight breeze, his dehydrated body balanced
on a wire like a dizzied trapeze artist losing
his momentary balance, his talon lifting
slightly, enough for the current to jump
the synaptic gap like touching
the grey steel band around the hole
in the heart of the cartoon man
in the kid's game Operation.

His nose lights up red, an alarm buzzes.
He spontaneously combusts, a ball of fire
falling, flapping. We've all burned
our hair once—that smell. His blazing

body licked the dead grass alive in flame.

"Buzzard Starts Fire."

The irony is his too burned

body is not even palatable enough

to be eaten by his own mirrored kind.

Playground Rules

When I get thinking I have it all, Mr. College Professor, I go
to visit my wife teaching elementary Physical Education. Every hour
the kids are spilled into her gymnasium like a box
of six week old kittens after having been manacled to desks and filled with starch
in the lunchroom. Today they are playing tag: "It-not It."

"Seems like an antiquated game for a bunch of computer-generated children."
Then she reminded me of the rules. "No one wants to be 'it.'
'It' has a disease and is contagious but can only pass
on the disease through human contact. The players
ridicule 'it,' make fun of 'it,' taunt 'it.' Watch, the girls want

to have a base, but they are reminded, there is no such thing
as base. The lead boys set boundaries and play within a semi-reasonable
distance and those who stray outside of reasonable limits
are cheaters—people don't want to play with them.
Oh yeah, no touch backs after you've been 'it;' 'it' can't affect
a 'just been it' immediately, because that person knows the wound of 'it.'"
I sit in awe. A lecture from first graders. "Next, we'll play
freeze tag. Same concept. Except there's a 'main-it' and multiple 'minor-its,'
but 'it' allows the 'non-its' to crawl between the frozen, the 'minor-its,' legs to free them.
Teaches compassion and enemies and who to trust, and best of all, to
cover your crotch when people crawl between your legs." I laughed. Her whistle
broke the air and the children meandered into the line. Roger was last. He had
    been 'it' last.
Roger waited smiling. I was confused. Why happy about being 'it?' She whistled
again and Roger ran full speed to the center of the playground and slapped
the Cottonwood tree. The class yelled "it" in unison. I was out of my element.

72

I looked for an explanation; my wife paraded the first of the line into the building;
the tail
of the line followed. I caught Roger, "What was that," I slapped the air. "That's the
'it' tree. Don't want to be 'it' all night, so we give 'it' to the tree." He popped
a hot Tamale out of a box and offered me one and I took it like communion even
though his hands were dirty. I sucked the cinnamon and looked back to the center
of the
playground to that great Cottonwood, the single tree on the playground.
'It' stretches out of the center of the earth like an antenna, a mouthpiece
of the clairvoyant, the arms of fate and absurdity. Each night 'it' stands
alone as black grackles blend beyond sight in 'its' arms with night. 'It' weathers
storms; 'it' palms the snow; and 'it' clings with 'its' feet to the soil like a
mandrake root.

'It' is a wooden Christ, a green-headed Prometheus. One morning the sun will pull
himself over the horizon and spy the tree, a tragic hero
who has fallen and become a God through death and all the burden
'it' takes with 'it.' "Next time I'll tell you about the girl's step on the slide."
Roger adds.
I look so far into his innocent eyes that he shares his secret. "All the steps,

except one, are raised with lines, that step third from the top is circles."
He points very exactly. "If you step on 'it' and are a boy, you turn
into a girl." He raised one eyebrow challenging me. "Does it work," I teased.
"No one's ever stepped on it. We're not stupid, Mr. Yarbrough." He pulled
his pants up and opened the door to the school and 'it' swallowed his body whole.

Teaching *Gilgamesh* to College Freshmen

See them inspect their limbs and size up
their intellects, mirroring themselves against
these archetypal ancestors. Two-thirds a god,
one-third human they picture themselves,
their heroic stories honed into stone walls. They create
their double and let the two contend.
                                    The girls wiggle
their thighs against desk chairs as the prostitute
seduces the stormy-hearted beast into consciousness.
The young men stride with Enkidu into Uruk to find his shadow.

Embrace and kiss and embrace and kiss again.

They smell the forest like a cedar box opened
with Pandoric curse. Hear death's rattle
and weep until their sockets are dark
and bleeding, for Enkidu must die, but Gilgamesh,
the gifted, must not.
                        They sit resolved and staunch
as Gilgamesh descends into the dark waters searching for the
How-the-Old-Man-Once-Again-Becomes-A-Young-Man plant.
They rejoice in his finding and relax and sleep, but fail
to suspect the simple serpent who slithers away with stolen
thorny agelessness.

"There are many pleasures before you weep;
embrace and kiss and embrace and kiss again," I say.
But the truth they've disturbed is their own mortal sleep.

His First Nativity

Newly married, York and Kat's first nativity sits
on their coffee table, type cast out of a toy chest
from York's Grandfather: all the siblings' leftover archetypes.

Joseph and Mary are Barbie and Ken in tattered
clothes. Mary is still pretty and fit for just having
birthed a savior. Appropriate, the mother
of Christ should be a looker; God's no slouch.
Joseph is standing smiling, strangely aloof, surprisingly accepting
of his immaculate miracle, despite his lack of true fatherhood.

The center wise man, York had named him "Frankincense,"
is Darth Vader; he has that grid across his face hiding
Fate: perhaps cloaking Christ from seeing the coming cross,
perhaps already trying to turn Jesus to the Dark side.
Shrek's Donkey even looked suspect. I ponder
if he might even be the Pawpaw of the ass Jesus
was to ride into Jerusalem in the Triumphal Entry
that got all the Pharisees in a huff.

God has a plan for everything.

Donkey was supposed to make people mad,
just like the legged serpent was purposely
placed in the garden to eventually slither, just like
Judas had to betray Christ and hang, like a stringless puppet,
a worthless cash of coins shining under his carcass. Where

would we be without God's carefully concocted crossroads?

I sat silent and took a drink of my eggnog laced with whiskey
and faith and I thought I heard the little voice of God rise
from the cradle, coddling his newfound innocence, wiggling
his new human toes, practicing, strengthening his original
cry from the wilderness, an infant reminding us how much
we need him, or—as Mary pulls him to breast—he needs us?

Floating the Comal River with Grandpaw
the Day After He Found Out Jenni was Pregnant

The water's always cold, but Father always puts
his tube in to float the Comal River. Two Schlitz
to the flume. That's where we always worry we'll
lose him. He insists on going, old man
with sons and grandsons and granddaughters.

He prepared as much as anyone can for a waterfall.
He even threw away his cans: butt up,
prone, feet pointed, until white-water
dumped him at the bottom, and his head,
skull and melon over light skin and winding
intellect, hit tight against a stone.

Nature hadn't moved it for two
thousand years. Why should he?

His foot caught in a crag, face down
with years of water curving over him.
A line, blood red, started downstream.
Jenni fought upstream and pulled his leg
and set him upright and stuffed
his body back into the rubber tube, holding
her new Oktoberfest T-shirt over the cut, red spreading.
Then, she carefully directed him downstream consoling him,
"That was the worst part, Pawpaw. The rest is easy."

"That's what you think," he laughed.

Those Winged Men

I wonder how Adam felt facing Eve,
her words and disobedient mouth
wrapped around the red apple?

Each second must have seemed a decade
for those winged men
who chanced to see their Icarus fall:
embraced, heads thrown back, strong throats,
some even belly-down
on thundering clouds, reaching for his feet,
watching him grow smaller and smaller still.

I wonder how Eve must have felt leading
Adam by the hand across the wilderness
in his itchy new clothes toward his plow?

Because I Wrote It Down

Fry the over-medium eggs and flip
the salty slice of bacon marbled
with its indecision to be fat or lean
because this lemon morning is going to last.
The clock's forever-arms are crucified at 9:15 am
because I unplugged the clock and you
are still asleep, still nude under
the white down comforter. You don't know
yet that you are late, but that it doesn't matter,
because I already called you in sick
and the kitten, Cowgirl Jessie, has had her half of a can
of seafood soufflé and is back asleep,
or that I put your tomato juice, Worcestershire,
and lime in the refrigerator with cracked pepper and a stalk of celery,
and the vodka is on ice, or that
you have a massage at two and I'll drive
you there and wait. Don't worry.
The only thing I have forgotten is
yesterday and tomorrow because neither
exist; I have stolen eternity from God
for a day and I can relax in the forever
of now because I wrote it down.

She Said It Might Improve our Marriage If I Vacuumed

I didn't want to vacuum anyway; I hate
the noise and the horrid sucking power
our particular model has; it scares me, afraid my
soul may somehow end up in the dust chamber.
I started in the closet, which was defiant
because she told me to start in the living room.
Are there rules to vacuuming? First rattle
out-of-the-bag, I tried to nip by a pair
of red silk panties without moving them,
but they shimmied over, and quick as a sixteen
year old in heat, they jumped the brush and threw
the belt. I said, "Dammit," like my mother
had taught me for domestic mishaps, and I
stomped it off and flipped it over, unscrewed
the head. I freed the panties and held them up.

I picture her hips pointing, filling out the space against
the silk, round and firm, and the V that disappears. I smiled.

I turned on the vacuum with renewed spirit and went
full speed over a bra. I repeated the 'off,' the head,
release and held the bra and pictured her breasts filling
each cup. By the end of the day, I had vacuumed
a thong, a strapless bra, cropped a silk negligee
just above the thighs and even dropped
the cleavage line in a blouse. She said

it might improve our marriage if I vacuumed
as she slammed the door two hours ago. She
probably doesn't know it, but she's just
created some new domestic god who now
understands housewives and desire;
It's all about the pleasure of vacuuming, let me tell you,
and you can blame her for letting the secret out.

The Great Cottonwood

When we're older
the trees grow like mushrooms
toward some quick finish,
puffed up and proud.

My father's house has no tree in the yard;
the great cottonwood fell
last spring in a violent storm,
ripping ripened wood
from the earth and
lay awkwardly, its hands
behind its back,
face down;
the smell of the turned soil
ascended from its tangled feet,
and the teaming albino insects
rushed back into the earth.

I filled the hole with zinnias and marigolds.
I replaced the fallen cottonwood with a
bed of fleeting colors.
That is easier to bear.

Putting "It" in "Its" Place

Two nights ago my wife slept in the other room;
didn't say what "it" was exactly and I didn't ask.
I haven't felt "it" in a long time.

"It" sits in the middle of the playground waiting
for recess while "not its" trade up the batting order.
"It's" the girl's step slumbering at night on the slide, or
spending her summers tanning on the blue see-saw,
lock-rusted, spread wide open in repose for Spring.

"It" is the abhorrent object indescribable: Cousin It,
King's clown of the sewer murdering our children,
the smell in the kitchen that crawled behind the refrigerator.
Tonight, I am "it," the tagged one, spouseless in our king-sized
boat of a bed looking for the shore. Or is "it" the absence
of her, the mechanism of the morning alarm to remind
me she's not here; is "it" the air she usually occupies? Maybe,

she took half of "it," or all of "it," into bed with her,
carelessly letting the cat drag "it" under the bed
to bat "it" around wildly, chewing "it" in "its" cat-clean mouth,
eventually even curling around "it" like a sparkling prize.

Or is "it" here beside me waiting permanently, quietly
crawling out of bed, that noise in the dark hall
I just heard like some hungry nothingness waiting
for me to lose my vigilant watch to give way
to indifference consumed by "it?" I want "it" back

in the medicine cabinet, capped in "its" bottle, "it" safely
circling my finger never finding "its" tail, never beginning,
never ending, too busy with "ourselves" to worry about "it" tormenting me.

Rosa Parks

You tell me my ebony skin is like kilned ivory
shiny and honed smooth by Jim Crow who keeps me
in my place. And you tell me that my music is too
sad for your white soul, yet you digest it like a meal
and ship it to England and disguise it in Rolling Stones
or gyrate it into the hips of a snarling Memphis boy. You tell
me my place is at the back of the bus where I can sit with
my own kind, even though you often leave me standing in
the cold Alabama winter after I pay, telling me you're "full-up."

I bet that bus driver thought he was just going
to have another drive under the mesmerizing
drone of his everydayness, his rearview seeing only white.

Well, today *I'm* full-up. Today I am tired of eating Crow
and providing your music and tending your children
and stitching together the fabric of your souring souls. I think
I'll rest these two hundred years of oppression right up
front so everyone can see my ebony skin is like kilned
ivory: heavy and hard but willing to mold a path through
the wilderness for my children to freely follow.

Tiresias

For Lee Weldon

Blind, groping blind. Imagine that:
relying on a boy to accurately account for the flights
of birds, or to describe the entrails of the refused sacrifice,
or to guide him mathematically to the market to get his leaves
of tea and lamb and figs. What fun

is discussing the rain he already knew was on
its way or the failing olive crop and all
those sticky footed flies? There will always be
the temptation to make a face at a blind man
or rudely just to look away. The Seer's

curse is not his knowledge, but his cursed knowing
what is done cannot be undone. There
he sits, trapped in his own labyrinth, androgynous,
counselor and healer, soothsayer and sage who can't
even comb his own gray hair. His clocks

are useless, but still he tinkers and holds one ear
close, wanting to understand what makes nothing
tick its teeth wheels in mindless circles.
Does he even know his house around him
is sunflowers, sunshine, and bright and squeaky yellow,

lemon air and mornings like red beets
until hot afternoon dies red blood

poured into black? Bury him in a Plathian
shrine, that fated sarcophagus that he may see
with his dull eyes the sky that reels

above him. Wrap him carefully with cloth that
is soft but already grows stiff and tight. Curse him
for his horrible gift of knowing all and nothing.
Even wrapped away clean, we'll call on his mouthpiece
to hear his simple solution: all ultimately is tragic.

Protesting Plath

I'm glad I didn't have to stand
in the cornucopia ear of my one-legged hero
trying to rebuild him, or feign
interest in his dancing bees moving
as one crawling flesh. Honestly, killing
oneself really shouldn't be *that* tedious. In fact,
the two meteors in the next room
should have been impetus enough. Didn't you
figure out in Boston after three martinis
that Sexton was crazy, too. Not
the best poet to compete with in suicidal one-upmanship.
Granted, what confessional doesn't want
some poetic horse to whisk her off to perfect
or who can deny the power of the pretty broken girl as the mouthpiece
to female clairvoyance? I'm sorry, I'm just
trying to help settle your tummy
and the sick of being you. I know anorexia is not
about food and your kidneys are aching; it's the only way
to become the food of your mother's voice; deconstruct her. Well,
now you've gone and done it, your
brain is unwound outside your skull
for all the critics to peck, a she-Prometheus punched
out like a paper doll, for stealing selfishness
from the Gods and offering the next batch of poets
over to self pity like a pharmaceutical loaf.

Didn't Pinocchio Know?

Didn't Pinocchio know
all the real boys wanted
to be him, living
in a marionette maker's house
with a magic cricket confidant
sneaking out with the bad
boys, asses ears
on dangerous duties, fresh
in his journey to becoming
a *real* boy, instead
of just some flesh
figure on strings
following everyday rules?

Catch and Release

for York

The sea rolls under the pillow of night; outside
waits the dawn. Those boats
large at port; twenty-five miles out are toys. This

afternoon we watched as our boy held up his Red
Snapper, tall as he, hanging mouth to tail
from shaking arm; he was still weaving from the rocking
boat. The scales were stacked pink fingernails. The fish's
horrible open eyes were punched out blind
from being pulled to the surface too quickly. Why

did that fish wandering that ocean floor
that day decide to eat that piece
of squid precariously bobbing? Someday

my son will slide his scales into that salty sea
and test his infant gills, gliding
his silver future across the sandy floor: a fin,
a tail, and then nothing except
the hollow ring of a conch to tell
the world he's caught his destiny and
not to pull him from the depths too quickly.

War Like a River

Somewhere in the aspen, she nuzzles
the soil like a snail,
chasing the scent of autumn
under the thin tin sheets of colored leaves:
rust and corn and clay,
and grows like a rumor,
joined by a roadmap of relatives,
nourished by snowflakes and icy streets.

Once mature, she can dislodge even the most secure,
scoop out canyons and split mountains,
swell on the six o'clock news,
move houses and farmers in aluminum boats
like sticks and paper pushed against concrete curbs.
The silent worker, the silent maid,
gathering the mouths of civilizations, dirty and unkind,
into a pool of salt and water and bottomless floors.

On A Run I Figure Out U.S./Eastern Relations

The earth here in Dallas is dry. The soil
is cracking the size of black electric chords.

On a run, I stopped and picked a dead stick
from the foot of a Pecan tree. I stuck the stick
and probed the crack; I was like some gorilla
on TV fishing for consciousness. I couldn't feel
the earth against the stick; curious, I let
the stick go. It disappeared and was very black
wholly gone. Crack of all cracks gone.

The rest of my run, I picture some bright-eyed woman,
face framed in a pomegranate sun, adjusting
her Sari looking oddly into a curious crack
by a wild Hazelnut tree, when a stick jumps
from the crack to smack
her square like a red dot marriage.

The earth is hollow and round. We don't know
what simple actions can conjure. God, this
is some long drought and the earth is cracking all over.

Why can't Lakshmi shower brides with coins,
and Ramadamadingdong with Cheezus and crackers while bustin'
big to a rub-a-dub big Budda belly rub?

Perhaps it is time that the prophets unite; call

a truce and declare the earth is round and we'll
all uncurl from this ancient linear history
and began to wonder why so many peaceful
prophets still have us wandering these deserts
always warring over one lost sheep, when
the rest of the flock is just fleecy fine.

Little Sister's Red Dress at the Wedding

Who would have known that just below her
resting hands, under that red taffeta, the child
was just spinning herself, snuggling into
the wall? She thought it was, perhaps, that
piece of unleavened communion that caused
that taste, or nerves from singing in front of all
those people. But even
as the white dress trailed past, swirling her
dreams, cells were rapidly rushing and splitting,
reading their maps, constructing during
her private vows. No one's first words to her
were congratulations and really, it is
so much more miraculous, now.

He Once Asked Why I Teach Mythology

For Jerry Barton

Jerry was at his grandson's second birthday
when the spidering cancer first dulled his view.
He said there was a pungent smell just
before his head hit the concrete and his
blood spilled out in a rich-red puddle.
His thumb bent back to his forearm. Rather exacting.

He wanted to treat his newly found cancer like a textbook
existential chasm. So, I bravely let him drive
the new golf cart, the doctor had told him "No." On hole
five, I mentioned to him that my in-laws were coming for Thanksgiving.
He teased that they may be worse than his
predicament. He gave me a simple recipe: "Wake
at four-thirty, make a Bloody Mary,
and prepare the fresh plump turkey rubbed
with poultry seasoning and fresh tarragon. Stuff
your skull full of postcards, of smells, of the glorious
moment. Then, make love with your wife passionately
enough to wake the hibernating loins of her parents in the next room."

We laughed, and he almost drove the cart into
the concrete creek. I stood on my beer can like
a little god before I teed off to seal the moment.
He fainted on the twelfth hole. On the way home,

he made me drive by the concrete Christ
in the cemetery. He read the base of the statue.
"Translated, it means 'God, why hast thou forsaken
me?'" he confirmed. I finally fell

into that textbook chasm beyond all those stars
snapping in Camus' small sky. We drove home.
I helped him to the door at his house.
The hydraulic hiss of the piston shut against me.

Alone inside, he must face his mirror Minotaur
who is reeling and snorting and rushing
through the map of his labyrinthine mind, the unknowing
beast nearer and nearer until he is face
to face, staring into his own wide-eyed bestial mortality.

We've been trying to outwit
the gods since we could swim and crawl
and babble and form from clay. Religion and myth
are as certain as cancer. We will all wake some morning
dead, to our Gorgon mother with writhing head
and slotted green-ice eyes. To stone will we
return. We will all calmly be rowed certain
in that ancient wooden boat, honed smooth,
polished only by human handling evanescing from body to soul
as Charon's fingers' bones click our teeth to take
the silver coin from beneath our babbling tongues.

Be Careful What You With For, Little Girl

"What's stupid literary analysis for anyway?
 I just want to move," Julie said.
She pumped her hips on "want" and "move."
There are times when silence is best.

Be careful what you wish for little girl.
You may just get to be as big as you
thought you wanted to be. First,
you should prepare for your journey:

alienate your family; then, confirm
an animal as your new BFF.
Dogs are always good to run
away somewhere over the rainbow.

Second thoughts? Too bad. Screen door's smacked
shut, your home-sweet-home's twisted up in a tornado
and dropped into a color-filled, little-people patch.
You'll need new shoes when you arrive; a journey requires them.

Red sparkly ones always stir up the town.
Bask, because suddenly, you're bigger
than even the mayor, got a key to the city, and
an endorsement from the Good Mother. Still, there's

always that catch; your journey is just beginning. Just
stay on the straight and narrow and everything will be

fine, but look left and right, pay attention
to crossroads, and remember to pick up some tools:

get some brains for logic, a heart to feel, and a badge for courage,
even if—inside—you're really still scared. Road Trip! Stay
away from drugs, especially when you see your final
destination; there are those who want to see you fail.

Big cities always offer unique challenges; they can
change as quickly as a horse of a different color.
"Nobody gets somethin' for nothin'," either. So,
you'll probably have to talk to God. [It was inevitable.]

God's pretty scary, too, a figurehead speaking out of fire.
And God, damn him, he'll send you on that one last duty
—a small task for a God—but a mountain for a mortal. It will require
a trip deep into the woods, off the path, and you'll probably

meet some flying monkeys. Textbook Rule: fight evil
with good. Try water instead of fire to melt away your enemy.
Those you save from slavery will thank you with a key.
And then, just when you think you will be the hero,

you'll find out your God is just man's mirror-image feared. You'll find
that hearts and brains and courage must be cultivated; you'll emerge,
and instead of red ruby pumps, you'll find slippers silently sliding
an ageing sage searching for no place but home.